The
Sensitivity
Of A Man

Prose, Thoughts
and Poems About
Life, Love, Living
and a Man's
Search to Find
Inner Peace

Everett R. Hubbard

Outskirts Press, Inc.
Denver, Colorado

ALL PRAISES
DUE
TO THE

FATHER

WHO ART
IN
HEAVEN

WITHOUT **WHOM**, NONE OF THIS
WOULD BE POSSIBLE

THIS BOOK
IS DEDICATED
TO MY
WIFE

EILEEN HUBBARD

FOR HER LOVE AND SUPPORT
IN BELIEVING IN MY
DREAM

IN
MEMORY
OF MY
MOTHER & FATHER

**JUANITA M. HUBBARD &
CLAUDIE HUBBARD JR.**

WITH LOVE
TO MY
DAUGHTER,
MY
HOPE AND INSPIRATION

TIFFANY M. HUBBARD

MY BROTHER
FOR BEING WHO HE WAS

FRANKLIN L. HUBBARD

AND TO MY SISTER
FOR BEING WHO SHE IS

YVONNE L. MORSELL

Table of Contents

I

There is never darkness, beloved,
only light.
And what shines either enables us to see,
or if we choose,
blinds us from the truth.

<u>The choice is up to you.</u>

Introduction

The purpose of this book isn't to preach about one thing or another, it is only meant to explain the sensitivity of a man, and the things in my life that affect every aspect of my being, through my experiences with **GOD**, nature, myself, and people, touching upon your heart my reason for living …

What I'd like for you to do is to sit back, relax, and read as I recite my life through these words.

Feel the joys and pains of my conception to manhood, as this infant of a man takes hold of his umbilical cord to Life.

The Opening

"All things are relative to Life, and not to the manifestation of man's words"

I don't consider myself as the author of this book. To me, I'm just an interpreter of the lessons Life has shown me.

Even though I form words of my own choosing, making the experience personal in the light of me, I still view my writing as a painter would view his or her drawing ...

Whatever it is I see or feel, even through my mind's eye of imagination is only an interpretation.

This means that my writing doesn't come from me, but rather, *through* me.

Its energy existed long before I experienced the event or wrote these words.

I'm just a vehicle through which Life makes herself know ...

And through my living, Life gains another perspective, translating my experiences into her own point of view, seeing through my eyes the space that lies between me and possibility, where decisions drawn between the lines of need and want carries my spirit to a level of understanding hidden in the solitude of my soul ...

The end results are points established before I make the move.

Conclusions I build upon that govern the path I walk, the choices I make, and the morality I base those choices on, interpreting from my lessons on living the wisdom of Life.

My Life

I was born into this world with no guarantees, given as my only means of survival the gift of Life.

A life not to be reflected or looked upon as a novelty or thought of as an idle word, but a gift given to me to be lived through my spiritual needs and intentions.

Integrating with the oneness of nature, assimilating with the wholeness of being, standing steadfast in my triumphant cause, emulating **HE** whom my spirit knows to be true.

For the foundation of existence begins in the heart and soul of **GOD**, and because of this, I know to live is to *act* upon being alive.

And what I do with my life becomes a living example to everyone that connects to its content, making me a part of you, you a part of me, and us a part of **GOD'S** eternal love; for we're all blessed creations, sent to this world to make a difference, and our presence plays an important role, a role that shouldn't be taken lightly, but instead, lived righteously.

II

In order to for me to move forward, I must understand the present, and in doing so, taking upon myself the challenges of conquering my current condition.

The Sensitivity of a Man

The sensitivity of a man speaks to you as a soulless victim of his own insecurities.

Scarred by a tradition that justified my fear of feeling and my inability to show love, I wander through the circumstance of my existence, trying to find my way back to the road of righteousness.

Marred by my misconception of the American Dream, I lie dormant in the hallways of drug-infested rat holes, rejecting not only the light of truth, but even the warmth of the sun, as my nocturnal instincts take over my godly ways, creating the savage you see scouring the streets ...

But there's a voice inside of me; a voice that speaks with the confidence of **GOD'S** conviction, as my spirit humbles itself to the sermon coming from the mount of my mind ...

"Yea, though I walk through the valley of the shadow of death, I will fear no evil; for thou art with me."

I ... even the me inside of me understand now as I've never understood before, that **GOD** lives within—*within even me.*

So, I, as a **Black Man**, must rise.

Rise above the base desires of my carnal cravings to see the vastness of my creation. For I am the father of humanity, who brought forth from the loins and wombs of my ancestors righteous men such as Abraham, kings such as David, wise men such as Solomon, and prophets such as Daniel, and last but not least, the King of kings, **Yeshua**, who you call *Jesus*!

Yes, these are the men who emanate through these dry bones that were cast aside by the ignorance of my rage as I tried to seek refuge from my identity, encountering all the inequalities that equate the total sum of my desolation.

For I have ceased to be for the sake of being, destroying myself from within.

Broken Down

"A job well done," is the sinister cry of the vile beast that stands on two legs as he/she systematically destroys the threefold nature of me ...

My ***body***, beaten down by the poverty of a prolonged cycle of hatred, my ***soul*** has torn itself from the ties that bind my benevolence.

As my misdirected energy becomes polarized within the nucleus of my ***spirit***, I seek solely to obtain for the acquisition of self-preservation; for I have become removed from Life's eternal order of ... ***cohabitation***.

The Picture

Appreciate for a moment the loneliness that accompanies me ... a man left to stand without a nation.

Isolated from a definitive meaning to model from, I am forced to identify with the very society that holds me prisoner, locked in a subculture where life is reduced to something less than livable ...

Here, I compress my existence into 24 hours of a day.

Concerned only with my basic needs, I have become a living example of the failure I fought so hard not to be ...

It is in this state that I'm asked to draw a portrait of myself: *a portrait cast in the reflection of he who persecutes me.*

Self-inflicting by pen in hand the suicidal project of conceptualizing a face: *the imagery of a man depicted as something other than the features that bear my resemblance ...*

I now have colored contacts in place of my dark brown eyes, bleached skin to enhance the prospect of my success, and with chemicals in my hair pressed so close to my mind, I've limited any chance for an escape of identity.

For self has been bargained away for the price of acceptance, making my picture of me ... a **Black Man** ... a forgery.

Appreciate for a moment the loneliness that accompanies me ... a man left to stand without a nation.

The Illusion

I see through eyes shaded by the rose tint of ridiculous, obscuring my view from the gloom that looms over me.

Blinded by the madness, I wander through the maze of wanna-be-like-them, forgetting who I am as a person and remembering only the pains of what being a **Black Man** is—*I'm now traveling in disguise.*

Camouflaged in a sea of whiteness, I appear as a black dot plastered into the framework of a scene already happening, pleading to the status quo, trying to get an honorable mention to finally settling for just a nod of appreciation—*my body shakes uncontrollably*—for the nature of my soul cannot believe the submission my mind forced upon my spirit.

I have violated myself by reason of assimilation, reducing my existence to its lowest common denominator.

I have become the reproduction of a man struggling to be seen …

I know in myself my identity, but I still see the imitator imitating me.

Like a puppet controlling the puppet master, he has placed the strings of survival around my neck, strangling the very breath of my determination.

I'm suffocating from lack of concern, and because of this, I'm forced to separate myself from pride in order to survive ...

Don't think I don't understand.

I watch the TV screen of Life replay the atrocities befallen my people and me every day.

I hurt, beloved, I hurt so deeply, and the only one that can appreciate my pain is you, and the only one who can understand my suffering moves through you ...

FATHER, I stretch forth my hands for the comfort and guiding support, for the inspiration **YOU'VE** given a world that reveres me as its enemy.

Place into my woman's heart the love necessary for her to endure my misery.

The Question

Will a man choose for himself what is truly righteous, or is it the nature of a frightened man's fear to alter the course of his destiny to avoid the chance of seeing what GOD'S goodness is trying to reveal?

Honesty is the only way I can bear witness to this question, and within the nature of my spirit, one fact remains as a conscious reminder, and that is that the integrity of a man is measured by the honesty he shares with himself.

Therefore, I have to ask myself.

What lies have I set before my soul?

Open the Door

Gambling, alcohol, and drugs became the focal point of my self-destruction, as the liberties of freedom left me in a prison made of illicit things.

Locked in, I found no peace, but there was nothing holding me, for in my hand I held the only key.

In the grandeur of life there are so many things that played into my equation, and seeing with eyes of a material world, I've missed most of those remarkable things.

Apparently, for reasons I'm too afraid to face, I decided not to use the key.

Finding the Strength

The howling winds pass through my clothes as I walk the deserted streets of my mind.

Seeing the ruins of a beautiful life, I stopped to pay tribute to a time I once knew ... *my family* ... *two children and a wife.*

What once was a wholesome way of living now appears as a gem of enormous wealth.

Unattainable by me, my world has become a living hell ...

Nightmares are now a part of my conscious state as the limbo land of misery confines the strength needed to set my spirit free.

You see, it's not that I don't understand my problems, it's that I refuse to accept Life's demand to resolve them.

So, fearful of responsibility, fleeing from the family who looked to me, I found peace in a bottle written with my name ...

Alcohol, the river to a troubled man's soul, carries me to a place where family has no need.

I have no answers while living here, for solutions have left my mind, leaving me tired and so alone.

As for my wife ...

She's forced to leave behind her heart.

Picking up the pieces to our broken dream, she moves with the grace of a lonely swan swimming against the tide.

Set upon the journey I've forced her to travel alone, she somehow finds it in herself to look beyond her pain, and coming to terms with it, tears flow from a river she once thought was dry ...

"I still love him."

Her voice echoed softly to me in the wind as my heart soaked in the moisture of her tears, washed away all my troubles and fears.

And what came upon me ... the abuse ... the neglect ... the life I currently live became a turmoil that would break its own hold.

By my own submission, the bonds of my internal grief released their grasp, and falling at a rate unmeasured by man, I hit the ground with a clap of thunder as the earth shook below my feet ...

Upon my limbs I stood on solid ground.

Founded in principle and guided with the strength of a man determined to be free, I stood in the midst of **GOD** and my woman's love.

And with outstretched hands, I reached to the necessity that abandoned me, cradling in my arms Life, my woman, my children, my integrity, and there … right there, I found peace in the purpose of being a man.

III

*Life, without the guidance of **GOD**, compounds one's miseries, multiplying it by a pain that prohibits the heart from profiting from what was spiritually gained.*

Come Home

Never move pass **GOD** or yield to worldly conditions.

Rise above the way you're living, knowing that the turmoil surrounding your life isn't the way **GOD** intended you to live; for your emotions or addiction will find a way to justify the unjust …

Never fear the pain of change for you'll never know what the process of healing can do, or the finding of how far you are from you god self.

Speak to your spirit, for it knows, and in it lies your lasting need to salvage what's left of what you've chosen to leave behind, and that's the goodness that reminds your heart to live up to what **GOD** intended you to be.

And in your private moments of time spent alone—*where solitude meets with decision*—try not to answer your problems through the passion of your experiences.

But rather, answer them from the death of reason—*the whys that made you do what you did*—and the life you gained through understanding—*the wisdom you achieved after you did it*.

And with inward eyes, look deep inside your soul, seeing not for the first, but for the last time, a person bent on a worldly concept of living.

Come to Terms with Peace

Talk to yourself in the face of Honesty; share with your division the mortar that will bind your heart to your soul.

Allowing your spirit to be free, in-flight for a frontier far beyond this place and yet your body hasn't moved.

Where freedom can be found in the inner peace one finds in a new day … like a flower, nestled in its bed of soil, can find contentment even in its limited movement.

To be still, to hear, to feel, and smell, taking note of the finer things in life, seeing also the simpler ones.

Sight Unseen

I asked a question to a blind man the other day. *"How does it feel not being able to see, not knowing what a person looks like, unable to visualize physical beauty?"*

Tilting his head to the side then shaking it with disgust, he turned to my voice and said, *"Son, I think you should answer that for yourself, because I can see quite well.*

"To feel ... to touch a person's heart is what enables me to see.

Beyond the physical, a person appears to me through their spirit ... their inner face, the light that illuminates clearer than what sight sees.

"And what I see is more real than what your eyes show, for in the depths of what you perceive as darkness, the true face of one's image glows.

"And through their radiance their sincerity is what appears to me, placing in place the one vision your eyes can never see.

"So, to answer your question ... yes, I can see; I can see quite well.

*"But can **you** see me?*

*"Can you **really** see me?*

"I think not, because if you could, you wouldn't have asked that question."

Truth

As I materialize from the matter-of-fact to life—*which is my essence engineering itself through the realms of man's consciousness*—I search for a crack … a hole … any opening that will allow me to *ooze* my way out into a more tangible sense of being …

If I could just become a cell, I would have taken yet another step to my conception; for to be, I must conform to man's understanding of being.

Why can't his mind conceive and acknowledge me for what I am, just as he believes in **HE** that made me to be?

Because in my natural form, I live through the words of **GOD**, and my presence prevails far beyond the realm of physical.

"I am known as Truth."

A living essence spoken from the **POWER** that is and will always be; for **GOD**, with **HIS** majestic and infinite wisdom, has unselfishly blessed me with the will to live through man, allowing me—*over the millenniums*—to cultivate the hearts and minds of individuals lost in their own darkness.

And for all I give, I'm still not accepted or looked upon as being alive; for my life and the state that it's in … you can count as less than nothing, yet, even a zero has a symbol to represent itself.

As for me, man can only visualize darkness; a desolate space in his mind, barren and frightening.

But the fear he feels isn't of me, but rather of himself, whereby, negating me, he, in turn, cancels himself out from himself, extinguishing one of the most radiant illuminations existing in him and a chance to walk from the shadows of his own doubt into the light of knowing oneself and the reality of what his life truly is.

The Reality of Self

The therapy of loneliness brought to light the shadows of my fears, which revolved around the belief that my existence outweighed the essence of my being.

In that there was no quality in life outside the conditions I'd created, making my prerequisite to survival my ability to alter the course of it.

"I control, therefore, I am," became the theme to a badly composed composition on living, conceding to those words as my approach to Life and reacting through them for my own personal gains: *not realizing that all interaction reverberates an inner action.*

Therefore, if there is to be harmony in me, then I must be in tune to the universal law of cohesiveness, with its application being applied to the collective bonding of individuals in association with the ethical and moral codes of equality, and that no one is above or below these laws, including me …

Then … and only then … can I come to grips with the reality of reality, to face myself in the presence of my self-centered ego, coming full circle in actualizing my true purpose of being.

Life's Gift

We are creations as well as creators, each one of us comes from someone else, and through conception, Life has entreated herself in us, accepting as the trade-off our understanding of her purpose.

Her only hope is that we get it, which is the wisdom surrounding her sacredness and the whys that make us part of her whole.

We owe it not only to ourselves, but we also owe it to Life to understand how precious that is, and when someone asks you, *"How's Life treating you?"* you should say to them, *"You mean, how I am treating Life?"*

Because Life owes us nothing and we owe everything to Life, for she has given us all she can possibly give.

IV

Face your problems and disregard the pain.
Never lose your soul in search of a reason
to run away.

Homeless

Logic fails to reconcile the guilt I feel as I step over the bodies of homeless people living in the streets, men, women, and children, all of whom abandoned by society.

And when I take a closer look at my life, I find I'm only one step from their misery, so being that close to being destitute, can I afford not to recognize their plea?

Because one day that homeless person could possibly be me.

Enemy of Life

Life, in pursuit of herself, runs toward me, and I know not from where she comes, as every aspect of me stands in amazement, watching Life's frantic search for the remnants of her lost cause.

Confusion etched across her face reveals the conflict she has yet been able to understand; for the adversary of Life is an enemy called man.

Life's Need to Change

I, as a man who has come through the hardships of my past, still fall short in understanding.

Even though my travels have taught me the values of Life, I still carelessly neglect the most important lesson of all, and that's the totality of it all.

I have become desensitized to the injustice heaved upon my people, who ask no more from Life than what Life has to offer, to, in turn, become victimized for the salvation of their own souls …

I no longer recognize the face of a frightened child or the frustration of a father who can't feed his family.

As for the mothers?

They are the ones forced to bear the load, carrying the weight of over 400 years of oppression upon a back that can no longer support the family's needs, yet they still struggle … crying with tears of tomorrow for the pains of today their hearts have already hardened to.

Saddened from seeing life all too real brings a sigh to the ending of their day …

Check out your mind, brother.

Check out the missing pieces from a world you perceived to be suitable for life as it turns out to be a habitation occupied by burnt-out brothers, trying to recover from a state of mental paralysis. A condition brought upon by your own denial and your unfulfilled appetite for drugs, money, and sex in spite of your revolutionary rhetoric while you sit in your stupor telling me to free your mind …

Free your mind?

Free your mind from WHAT?

And please, don't answer the question by explaining the anatomy of your anal pursuit to prosperity; for the liberation of self follows that which promises freedom and hope of a better world for all, and not the ass for the sake of its hole, which can only seek relief from a little pink pill.

So, don't offer me a laxative.

Instead, peek into the world of a poor family's life and *then* you tell me how you spell r e l i e f.

For what ails their hearts extends to the evolution of our minds as our thoughts are quickly whisked away to a time and place where none of us can find rest …

What we're experiencing are the aging lines of existence as Time erodes the very youth of our once-proud and powerful people.

We are now finding ourselves subjected to Life's need to cleanse herself in order to preserve the beauty she has to offer ...

The finality of it all is the preparation for a new beginning, because the circle of Life can never be broken, nor can the lines of her diameter be changed, but all who make up her circumference have to be rearranged, transforming the mass within in order to bring about a change.

V

The art of simulation saturates our world with facsimiles of what could be, placing at our disposal replicas of a reality that stifles the imagination instead of enlightening it, changing the concept of logic by bending our spectrum of insight, creating an altered state of consciousness backed by the validity of a machine.

The Computer

What are we becoming in this world of micropro-cessing, the uncommon ground, linking that which is to the things that can never be as the computer cre-ates deceptions made from programmable thought.

Thought screened from the sensitivity of life, the compassion of love and the fondness of a friend, desensitizing our faculties by numbing the frailties of our emotions, allowing our minds to absorb the illusion as raw experience.

Removing the physical need of our bodies to in-teract with the consequences of our decisions, we are now finding ourselves suffering through the tragedy of Time's sequential search to find a me-dium to tick our seconds through, for we have given the computer power to govern our lives—

Reducing existence to a mathematical calcula-tion assembled and coded in a predetermined order, placing Life at the fingertips of our keyboards …

Take me back, take me forward, but please, don't leave me here, because here and now has passed and gone, leaving us in a suspended space in time—*a world unregulated by absolutes*—where reality has left the confines of the human mind, entering into a world of virtual madness, where the unreal becomes real and the obscene a sight to behold …

It's not what my mind can conceive; it's what a machine can make me believe.

I can no longer compensate for the acceptance of this as innovation closes the door to industrialized thinking, pink slipping manpower and substituting electrical energy as its sweat for labor while body and soul are dissolved by the creative force of … the computer.

GOD help us.

Complacency

I'm stuck in this web called complacency to satisfy who?

You?

Because it surely isn't me.

For without you, I'm boundless, without limitations, stifled only by your enclosure encompassing my world.

For without your walls my spirit would escape the confines of this humanized configuration you've dubbed reality, to encounter something beyond the physical comprehension of *Is* …

This *Is*, which I choose to call the third entity singular, isn't just the present, but moreover within the time continuum of the present.

Woven into the tapestry of our psychological world, it channels itself through the realms of possibility for the preservation of hope.

When in me, it works collectively with my innermost ambitions, instilling in me a life I only thought lived in dreams …

The visions in my mind, the thoughts of being there, and the acting as if I were ...

But unfortunately, your logic prohibits me from experiencing this side of Life, allowing pessimism to creep in, paralyzing my spiritual growth, thus, making me motionless just long enough for you to pour the fluid of complacency into my soul, creating in me the illusion of security.

Whereby, your way of living becomes a safe haven made from your so-called rational decisions ...

I hate the plausibility of it all, when conjecture is substituted for raw experience, encapsulating a situation into an add-water-and-stir scenario which most people can figure out.

In that, there *Is* no actuality to reality, only what you think it should be, never what it really *Is* ...

This, I call, the practical life, regimented into a fundamental routine of an ongoing cycle, beginning with the cadence of *hut, two, three, four, it's off to work we go*, and ends with a mechanical kiss and a good night, dear ...

But, alas, you're comfortable with that, and that's OK, not because I said so, but because it *Is*, and for that reason, you must understand there are thoughts in me which defy that comfort zone you live in ...

Thoughts that motivate a creativeness you won't always understand.

So, don't judge me during my episodes of what you call insanity, but rather, look inside yourself for that border person and then smile in what you see in me.

For I am … and that's all there *Is* to be for me.

Be Yourself

Coiled into the madness of a melodic dream, desensitized by the preconceived notion of tranquility.

I've closed the door to imagination, making me insensitive to the odyssey of creation.

Fearful of my condition, I/me try to manage the message, arranging in some logical form an answer I haven't figured a question to—*so people call me crazy*—making insanity synonymous with my views which are contrary to theirs, I'm forced to reduce my thoughts to a level deemed socially acceptable.

Spoon-feeding myself to satisfy those around me, I struggle to be understood by people who don't know themselves, compelling me to warehouse my creativity in the solitude of socialized control …

While rotting in this idle state of existence, I ponder the validity of it all; for I have relinquished my right to self-expression, denying my spirit the privilege to touch upon Life … my life … through the natural course of my existence and the creativity which grows through understanding and my need to coexist with that understanding—*not doing this, to me, is insane.*

I want to learn the song a bird sings, to hear the chimes of Life's enchanting melodies as she serenades her songs of love.

For I am a flower, plucked from the garden of **GOD'S** loving heart, and my needs must be nurtured by way of my interaction with the action of Earth's being, moving in unison to the harmonic cords of **GOD'S** creative energy as I walk proudly through the soil of my existence.

To Listen

Listen to me, beloved; hear the words that I speak.

For the weight of my existence weighs heavily upon my need to be understood, explaining something to you that is so vital to me ...

Just as a branch is broken from a tree, we have separated ourselves from ourselves, due, in part, to our lack of understanding and our inability to *want* to be understood, taking from the wholeness of one, leaving a sum we can never fully appreciate ...

The original beauty of that broken branch, which represents a person's life and ideas, contains leaves and seeds that will never be seen nor sown.

It will then be forced to wither and die for lack of nourishment ...

My nourishment ... your nourishment ... which is our ability to listen.

Always remember, we can never fully understand ourselves until we start listening to each other, because knowledge lives in all of us and our strength lies in the power of collective knowledge—*the key ingredient that complements our ability to comprehend*—and no matter how wise we may think ourselves to be, our bodies aren't surrounded by an ocean, nor are our minds as vast as the sea.

We can always gain understanding from each other, because it takes more than one branch to make up our family tree.

VI

The light of Love seeks not the heart that hides behind the shadow of despair; for Love doesn't want to find those who don't want to be found.

The Argument

I was standing at the window watching you walk away when something strange came over me.

Tears filled my eyes uncontrollably, overwhelming my masculinity.

At that moment, I felt as helpless as a baby, unable to nurture my feelings or understand this sensitive side of me ...

A hush came across my mind as I silently surveyed the thoughts I was having while the imbalance of my body swayed to the rhythm of my mindless binge of neglect.

Just then, the past whisked to the forefront of my mind.

Like a rerun, I could hear the words we exchanged in the argument we just had.

You walked out the door with the strength of broken promises and stood-up evenings.

Things I used to say that would heal your wounded heart are now words which have no meaning, forming sentences that bring no joy ...

You thought so much of me, and I made sure of that, for I promised you all in my power of pleasing that I would place your love above all, denying you for no one at all.

Instead, I was blinded by the night life.

Caught up in the whirlwind of syncopated rhythms and shimmering bodies as you sat quietly at home, removed from the good times I thought rang through my ears …

Good times, huh?

Yeah, that's what I thought I was having.

Partying until the break of dawn, dancing our lives away as my high greeted the morning sun.

Coming home to the question I was always left to explain.

What lie can I tell her today to make her pain go away?

I Know Now

Vast is the space that separates me from my missing link: *the person that brought me face to face with the love I thought was absent from my heart.*

I realize now that it was my arrogance veiled over my eyes as pride that concealed her love she wanted me to know, shielding my heart from the light she shined my way ...

The weight of my knowing this weighed heavily upon my soul as the flicker of Love's last light struggled to show me the darkness of my dismay.

Piercing through the obscurities of my neglect, I covered myself with the guilt of a disdained man's memories of his lies, slumbering my soul into a sadden soulful sigh ...

How can I touch her feelings when I can't be truthful to my own?

Speaking softly as I drifted to sleep, I quietly whisper those words, asking myself the reasons why

I failed her and the justification that wouldn't allow me to even apologize for the injustice of my deeds.

But in all honesty I knew the reason why.

I knew the reality that shined through me like a beacon of truth; for what was left of me didn't want to see the light that would bring happiness to my sorrow.

Nor could it bear witness to the closure I needed to answer why I miss her so …

I had nothing left that I wanted to give, for selfishness had consumed my passion, placing my heart aloft while my ego entertained itself below …

Guilt stands before me now in this dream, seeking refuge in the realms of this wretched soul.

It menaces me like a dark predator, pulling me deeper and deeper into the abyss of my senseless shame …

To know is to realize, and to realize is to accept responsibility.

I have to come to terms with the actions of my deeds.

Facing the man in the mirror, I must look into the window of my soul to find what's left of what once was an honest man … a decent man …

Help me, **FATHER**.

Help me to find my way …

Feeling through the darkness of my neglect, I find my way back to the origin of my shame, and seeing my woman's weakness from her battle with me, I struggle to keep alive the light that was left of her love …

Kneeling down beside her tired soul, I tried to breathe into her the breath of my passion, but her lips wouldn't open; for she had given up on trying to be a part of me, and instead of living a lie, she decided to let her love die …

Why did I let Ego drive me to this point to only push me over the edge?

Ego doesn't care about Love, it only *Eases God Out* by seeking pleasure through the infliction of pain, using me in a manner where only my selfishness could profit from its morbid game.

And now that I realize the truth, all I have left is the hurt I've caused her …

This can't be my consolation, finding solace in the damages inflected to a heart that wanted nothing more than my love.

For if this is to be the comfort for my contempt, then how do I bear the burden to this wickedness I've allowed to find its way into my soul ...?

Even in this dream I can't avoid the answer, for in every corner of my thoughts I see my fainthearted soul hiding behind its falsehoods, as the ravaging bird of truth strips away the life I lived as a lie ...

Standing uncovered, shivering in the cold air of Love's lonely chill, I reached into the chamber of my soul to clothe myself with what decency was left from my escapades of illicit sensations, but my spirit wouldn't allow me to find the comfort I needed.

I need to open my eyes!!!

I need to awake from this cruel nightmare that's made itself a part of me, but before I can find peace, I must first suffer the consequences of my cowardliness, and this dream is the truth I've ignored, for I have been caught between the lies of my living, and I have to answer for living those lies ...

I must feel what I made her feel.

I must know the silence of the unspoken words of neglect, as the toll of my broken heart waits lamenting at the gates of Love's judgment ...

While standing there, the whispering winds of my woman's love whirled about me as what was left of her love spoke to me through the version of a tearful lullaby.

I love you so much that your pain has become a part of me, and I can't live like this anymore.

You see life through eyes of pride, consumed by that which promises life without love; you've closed your heart to the risk that is taken to find a need to love.

Believing the world revolves around you, you have become stagnated by the conditions you've carefully encircled about you, carving within the murkiness of your shallow walls the word god.

Love doesn't exist because of you; it exists despite you, and because you've chosen to ignore this, your emptiness is a condition brought upon by your own denial, and your conceit is a scar that will never heal until you realize the untruth you've lived.

Gasping with the breath of a desperate man clinging to time, I awakened with the last tear of our painful past; for I know now that I love her … and the reasons why.

Me to You

I call upon that which sleeps inside you, for the nature of these words are only meant to compliment, defining in terms expressed by me the beauty that radiates the reflection of you …

A reflection seen in the light of my eyes, and in them, you'll see nothing in contrast to what I hope your heart feels, so … love me, beloved.

Love me as you would love no other and be not ashamed of your weakness.

Don't let independence separate you from passion, imprisoning your heart with the loneliness of your fears.

Let, instead, your heart touch upon that which your hands cannot feel, removing you from that which ego tells you isn't so.

For it is my love that I want you to understand, and with it, all the frailties involved in my emotions; for my strength plays a major role in my weakness, a power which is strengthened by my submission to your love.

And with a free will, I impart with you the charge of my affection, equaling the total worth of my soul ...

This, I lay at the feet of your needs to be created and recreated by the bidding of your dreams.

Timeless Love

I've touched desire moistened by the fluids of your love as the sweat from your body's tears ease down the crevice of your back, mingling with your sensual curves, clinging to that which your spirit shares with the physical part of me.

For our love … our deep, wet, passionate love waits … no … *lives* … for moments like this.

Moments that stop time, allowing it to lap itself in order to preserve the beauty our love has to offer, enabling us to see the future in our present state of being, making our love a timeless, ageless, wonder to behold.

VII

The masking of one's emotions is a crime punishable by its exclusion, taking from the heart its only means of communication, leaving the shell of the thinker to reason without understanding the feeling.

I Have to Let Go

I don't want to go there anymore … I'm tired, but I just can't help it.

I've become consumed by that which seems to have more control over me than I over myself, as my situation situates itself on the doorsteps of my tomorrow …

Unconsciously, I deliberate over the intensity of reliving the pain: *a pain which distance itself from my happiness.*

I have no say in the proceedings as my thoughts judge while I lie and listen.

Helplessly, in the arms of Memory, I'm taken to a place where Now never gets the glory it deserves: *a space where remembrances fight to be recognized in the form that they occurred.*

They struggle, pushing aside reality which seems to have never happened: *a blur of events that I move through without conscious thought.*

The automatic motion that allows me to function without focusing, to see without knowing what's in front of me, to speak without knowing what I've said …

Distant words talking through the hallway of my mind opens the door to the effect of what losing a love one can do.

The verdict's been handed down and once again in the stillness of the night/day—*it doesn't matter*—I look into an empty room to see me standing in a pool of memories, wading in the waters of forgotten wishes, or standing on the shores of lost dreams …

I've indeed moved through my yesterdays today, standing halfway into tomorrow, for time ceases to follow me until I let go of my sorrow, releasing a feeling I told myself wasn't there, trying to let go of the loneliness my heart chose to bear.

Moments

You want me, but you don't need me, because when you do need me, you won't take my hand.

Always remember, all that is yours is only for a moment, so grasp it to make all you want of me, everything you could possibly need from me.

I'm saying this to you because I'm offering you the key ... the key to my heart.

Take it ... unlock my time, allowing my moments to share this instance with yours; for our lives exist only in the moment, and this is all that is truly guaranteed us.

We must cherish this time and use it wisely.

So, don't take anything away from it; rather, add all you can to it, for Life's fulfillment begins with understanding that our relationship depends not only on the giving of ourselves, but the sharing of our lives.

With this comes the future, shaped and molded in the fashion of our deepest desires, orchestrated and conducted by the infinite wonders of our souls ...

Play the song of love into this heart of mine, breathing in me the passion of my own desire; for I know not my feelings unless they're mingled with yours, and together, our hearts will soar to heights of which no one can ever see …

Taken from the shared experiences we've stored in the chambers of our memories.

What Is Her Love Worth?

What is it worth?

The price I must pay to guarantee your love, the amount … the sum … the sacrifice that makes us one.

A question asked only I can understand.

A question which forces me to express myself as a man …

Though hard as it is for you to believe, I give to the spirit of our togetherness my undying love, offered as a token of my loyalty, assuring your heart I will be by your side just as the shore is to the sea.

Committed, undaunted, I stand with responsibility, taking on the challenges of life and living them through my love for thee.

Relinquishing the rights I possess as a single man, I share with you these moments in this space called a life span.

Reason

My heart compares not, nor does it want to examine, the deeper meaning of Love; for Love lives not in the logic of a thinking man's mind, but only in the passion of a feeling man's heart, and this heart feels deeply for you.

And the attention I pay to this emotion … this union … brings to light all which my soul desires and needs: *the tireless effort put forth and the time we've spent into the building of our dream.*

And in your hands I place the most priceless jewel of my worth, and that is my life, which means nothing unless it is lived with you.

I Give to You

Is it the sweet nothings that you want to hear or the reality of what my life really is …?

I'm sorry, but I can't be the vision of your dreams: *a kind of black/white knight you wish would sweep you off your feet.*

The truth of the matter is I work hard and long hours for a salary that doesn't match your dreams.

My clothes aren't the finest of wear.

I'm just a simple man, struggling within his means.

I would if I could shower you with diamonds and furs, but I can't afford those things.

But what I can give amounts to all the wealth I can rightfully share …

A penny to a dollar, a dime set aside for your needs, this is the method I go about providing for the provisions of your dreams.

The yachts and fine cars are but a flickering fantasy, but when I awake, I open my eyes to a life lived not for the fulfillment of those dreams, but for the necessity of our needs, and in that lies the worth of my determination taken from the experience planning brings.

So, sleep not in a world separate from my own, but let our dreams dance together; for our vision is a triumph to our endurance, rewarded by the aspirations we've shared in a common dream as we open our hearts to each other, sifting through the treasures of Life's possibilities.

Why Do I Love You?

It wasn't for the sake of my loneliness, my insecurities, or even my need to be cared for that led me to your love.

Nor was it a conscious mode I placed my feelings in.

Instead, it was an unquestionable reality my soul demanded.

A prerequisite to the only earthly thing that really is, and that is that your love is as important to me as Life's need to fulfill herself.

For my wants and desires revolve around my need to be your desire, just as my dreams are centered on the hopes of yours, which means biologically, psychologically, and spiritually, I have become a part of you, entwined with your body, your mind, and your soul.

And it is through our shared emotions that Love has now manifested itself, and it was at that moment that I'd truly realized I'd captured this feeling in a vessel called you.

And as that realization was being chiseled in the cornerstone of my heart, I could see Love look up through her eyes, wink at me, and smile to say … I'm yours.

Sea of Loneliness

Somewhere out there in the Sea of Loneliness,
somewhere there's an island called You.
And tucked away, tucked away,
tucked so neatly away is your heart in a cave called
Sim-ba-la-to.

There, guarded by your feelings
and protected by your emotions and fears,
lies your heart encased in a mold
made from your love-lost tears.

Patiently, your heart waits beating
to the rhythm of Life's lonely tune,
remembering the songs of yesterdays gone by
and the loves you once knew.

And here now am I, a man possessed by your
feelings which have taken charge of me.

Captivated by your love-lost spirit
that has traveled many miles across the sea,
settling in this heart of mine the intuitive knowing,
which brings me face to face with my reality.

I am compelled,
not knowing why or where this journey will lead
me to; for Destiny has made its choice, and it is
clear I must follow through.
Casting my love to the fate of the wind,
just as a fisherman cast his net to the sea,
retrieving that which I know nothing of,
which harbors all that could possibly be.

For the need to be loved is wanted by many,
but Love has chosen only a few,
so I feel blessed and honored
Love sees me worthy to fulfill my quest through
you.

With that, I must say good-bye to myself,
for to find you, I must leave a part of me,
that part which is too sensitive …
too sensitive for the perils of my journey …

And as I set sail from the port of my heart,
I turn to see my emotions ashore,
with the look of hope my return home
will bring them the love they've been longing for.

My feeling of caring, my smile of forgiving,
the humbling way my faith looks to **THE ONE**
above, giving **GOD** thanks and praise for giving
me the strength to search the sea for your love.

Confused

Our love has been customized into a kaleidoscope of conscious confusion, because I no longer knowingly know what you want.

For my fallacious art of assuming has clouded my perception, turning my thoughts into a multiple choice of chance with each guess pushing me further and further from you …

My beautiful, beautiful, **Black Woman**, it is you and only you I truly love.

Stop having me to guess why.

What's to a Relationship?

Since you don't expect anything from me, you're not threatened by me.

Therefore, what I give you receive freely.

But as your emotions heighten, your expectations will follow, forming stages of likes and dislikes, stepping-stones measuring the concern I show you, creating questions like, *how much do you love me?*

Forcing me to explain what words can never clearly say.

And what if what I say isn't enough, then what?

Will you downsize your emotions trying to equate them with mine?

I hope not, because everything exists in time, and the boundaries of that space shouldn't be regulated by expectations.

For to complement doesn't always draw lines to similarities; there are always variables between two points.

And within that space lies the uniqueness that not only separates us as individuals, but binds us together by the structual frame of our differences, which shouldn't limit our love, but expand it ...

Creating a multidimensional field, complementing and connecting our distinctions into a reciprocal cycle of completion, evolving in our personal lives through the understanding of our downfalls as seen through the eyes of our better half ...

Try not to examine my love, because in doing so, you will lose the virtues of its presence, setting aside the reasons that brought me near to your heart.

Tired of Proving

I can't pretend anymore, nor can my imagination continue to conjure the images of what I want you to see …

Far from my life and even further from yours exist our spirits longing to be together.

Divided by the furthest one's fears and nearest one's tears, our illusion of love makes the possibility of us being together an endless maze of mixed emotions.

Circumstances caused by your heart trying to find its way …

I keep asking myself … why should I continue to prove my love, sending my emotions to a side of Life left to deal with the source of your past pains?

I didn't create your sorrow, nor does my gender indicate the possibilities of what your past perceives me to be.

I didn't symbolize anything outside of what my heart has shown you, and the essence of that should not be trivialized or taken as some sort of condescending approach to you taking your clothes off.

I never asked you for anything outside of the affection two people should feel for one another when they're in love, and the desire of that cannot be fulfilled through a heated moment.

So, don't take me through that trip.

You forget that I was the one who shared your suffering when there was no ear to be found.

I was the one who caught your tears before they fell unnoticed to the ground.

And this is how you repay my love?

Thanks, I appreciate it.

I appreciate there is no appreciation in you, and I have walked so far in my search to find you that I've become lost in your anguish, and now your pain has made my heart its home …

You know it's funny.

I look upon you as you looked them now, and the reflection I see is the same mirrored image that made you cry, bringing upon me the same sadness I once saw in your eyes …

I guess the script has been flipped, turning inside out.

I've become victimized by the victim, leaving me shivering on the same cold corner I once found you ...

It's obvious you don't get it.

You felt my heart and through my compassion you entrusted with me your pain, allowing me to nurture your sorrow, not by taking away your suffering, but by adding to your affliction my eloquence of love which allowed your heart to heal, and moreover to understand what it was healing from.

And when the time was right to see in me a reason to love again ...

I am that express reason, and my presence speaks through that which burns the eternal flame of devotion, demonstrated by my willingness to challenge all that made your heart harden and not believe.

I need and want you because I love you ...

This is the simplicity of what I've been trying to tell you, and I can't make it any simpler than what I've said.

I am tired from my battle with you, and what my soul seeks now is rest.

But should my slumber be without you lying by my side?

GOD forbid; for I have fought too hard for my victory to be celebrated with you in the arms of another.

I must stand firmly entrenched in the foundation of everlasting, because I believe one day your eyes will open, and your look upon me will be like that of a newborn child, seeing for the first time what it grew to know in the darkness of its mother's womb: that my love for you is eternal.

And the finality of my feeling will never falter from the frailties of your forgetfulness; for I know one day you will remember.

And the thoughts you'll have will be the wishes I already hold gently in my hands …

Let go of what I feel?

I can't.

Try, I must, to maintain a path for you to find your way back home.

A Message to You ... My Beautiful One

A person poised with the elegance that only Grace crowns its most illustrious jewels has instilled in me a wondrous glow, shining softly the radiant colors of your smile ...

It is because of you my life is now complete.

From the shores of my wants to the vastness of my ocean of dreams, I have fulfilled my wish for happiness through the wanting of you and the needing of you.

My only hope is that you can sense the depth of my sincerity as these words echo from my thoughts so pure; for your love has cast its reflection upon this heart which seeks refuge for its wanting soul ...

I know now that my love for you helps me to understand myself, in that, the wholeness of me depends on my frail, fragmented emotions becoming chipped away by the experience of our coming together.

Forming a statue made from parts of my forgotten

feelings, creating the image of what my hopes could be.

This is the gift your love has brought me, an answer to my heart in search of its meaning.

A Conversation with Love

Imagine, if you will, after all the lying and game playing you've done; you wake up one morning and decide to change your deceiving ways.

You want to have and to hold in your arms true love: *a meaningful relationship that will stand the test of time.*

But before you can receive that which your heart desires, you must first convince Love—*a living entity*—to believe in you …

<u>**This is my conversation with Love.**</u>

I was walking along the shore on my favorite beach, feeling lonely and left out.

Thinking about all the wrongs I had done and the careless way I shrugged off my woman's love.

Becoming haunted by those images, I started casting stones to the sea, wishing in my heart I could convince her to love me, if for nothing else, just one more day ...

As the stones skipped across the water's surface, I found each one came skipping back to me.

How odd, I thought, as they parted the same path in their return.

Fascinated by the phenomena, I continued to play the game, but finally curiosity got the best of me and I decided to call out to my invisible playmate ...

"Who is it that throws back my memories?" "From what part of my past echoes to me from the sea?"

I received no verbal response, but instead, a stone I had not thrown came skipping back to me.

Panic-stricken, my first impulse was to run, but my legs wouldn't allow me to move.

So, hesitantly, I reached down to pick up the stone ...

I noticed it wasn't like the ones I had thrown.

Its appearance was that of nothing I'd known.

Its weight was that of a feather, but its density seemed to hold Life in itself.

Its surface was the softest substance I had ever felt, almost like flesh, as if it were alive ...

I stood there in the sand and wept as I cradled the stone gently in my hands, and as my tears fell upon its surface, a layer from its shell shredded, revealing an inner core ...

It wasn't a diamond or a pearl, or anything that could be defined as a jewel, but I knew it was precious nonetheless.

I couldn't make out its color, for even the light of the sun dulled its radiance.

I had to close my eyes and feel its glorious array as its reflection bounced off every bone in my body ...

Captivated in awe and enchanted by its splendor, I decided to appeal to it for an answer ...

"From where have you come?" I asked.

"From what source was your entrance to my life delivered?"

Still, there was no response, no utterance of words to answer my plea, but only the warmth that radiated from its glow, and in that I found peace ...

While reflecting on the pain I had caused my woman, I finally realized the meaning of the stone, and turning back to the sea, I cried out to its source, knowing someone or something out there was listening, and that's when the voice spoke to me from the stone ...

"Are you worthy to receive the gift of your own creation?

"Can you stand up to yourself ... upon the rock ...

upon the mount of your convictions and do what it is you know to be true?

"Caretaker of the Earth, sit down beside me and tell me what is it that makes you so sure?

"Explain to me this day the difference in yesterday, so I can understand how your heart can now be so pure ...

"Speak to me, and don't lie, because I already know the truth.

"I've lived my promise through you, and from your words she believed in me, only to have her hopes shattered in the search of your sexual needs.

*"And now you ask me to believe in **you**...?*

"Why?

"You tell me ... why ...?"

In the stillness of a moment, in a lifetime of tears, I bear witness that the power invested in me has shown me the way.

And from the deepest side of my emotions I ask of you to bring back the one principle needed to make my life complete ...

I ask of you to bring back into my life the dawn of my heart's creation.

And from the bowels of my existence, I will bring forth the bounty of your love, and through toil and tolerance, I will harvest from you the food necessary to sustain her soul …

Trust, commitment, and loyalty will be the feast she'll feed upon, and with her belly full, I will quench her thirst from the cup of our togetherness …

Listen to me, *Love of Life, Life of Love*, trust in the words I speak, for I've lost myself in myself and found reason through the absence of you.

Misusing your power, I capitalized on the nature of her feelings, knowing all along her weakness— *which is my own*—centers on our need for each other and each other for our needs.

Instead, I saw only my favor, finding happiness in a deception I so readily assumed.

Playing on this, I deceived only myself while locking out my heart from me, allowing deceit to be the caretaker of my soul.

Dragging out the charade, I cared more about my sexual victory than the love she was showing me …

This woman, this beautiful **Black Woman**, has laid before me a finding that has cloaked itself around the dismay that hampers most women from sharing their true feelings … honesty, pure and simple honesty.

Why is it so alien to me?

I ask myself with all that I have gone through, why haven't I learned the lesson?

And the only reason is that I refuse to see, and in doing so, I've refused to bridge the gap between true love and the surface of my physical needs …

This is my plea.

Clear of what I've said, unashamed of my weakness, I stand before you humbled with humility, as the whispering winds carry these words to thee … let not my echo vibrate as an irritation to your soul.

Please, I ask of thee, speak to me.

"It is not my will to deny the actions taken from your heart, for my life lives through the needs of you.

*"So, take care of her, **Black Man**, son of the week's end; for in five days the universe was created and on the sixth day time was specially spent toward the making of you.*

*"Be clear as to what this means, because for you, the chemistry of creation was reestablished, and through your pain, birth was brought forth: **the creation of another, already established, knowing all along the companionship needed to make your life complete … was already done …***

"Look not backward, nor tarry in the loss of your autumn leaves; for spring has sprung and from the seed planted in your heart, I have come forth.

*"Savor this conversation and allow your soul to live out what **GOD** has blessed me to bring."*

Selah.

XIII

*Be clear of what you look for from Love, making
sure your thirst for it doesn't drown you.*

The Recreation of Me Through You

Spawned from the nucleus of your never-ending love, I have grown to the 10th power of my physical existence.

Evolving … shaping … turning into a person worthy of the honor to have you by my side …

Life, even in her most simplistic form, has meaning now, because to love you is to understand the meaning of Life.

Not for the selfish desires of two people, but rather the knowing that we are two life forces in a universe filled with the vitality of being, which helps to bring about balance.

The buoyancy between the surface and submergence of Love's timeless existence, transcending and descending the heights and depths of our human emotions as we unwind and entwine to Life's lyrical tune, played out as a romantic dance to Love's everlasting tango …

When our bodies embrace, I feel a warmth that can only be felt through our spirits.

It's not just the lovemaking, beloved; for that is only but a plus added to the total summation of my love for you, because that which is truly Love can never be fully appreciated through sensation.

For sensation alone tends to overwhelm itself to finally suppress itself through its self-consuming desire to fulfill our needs, leaving us empty through the ritual of our repetitive passion …

No.

As for me, I stand before you as a testimony, testifying to the hearts of those longing to be felt and wanting to feel that true love does exist.

And it is through you that my lifelong ambition, my purpose, and my reason for being has been actualized, carried out in an order and measured into a physical component reborn through you.

The Message 1

This isn't a poem of poetic words running together to make sense of some literary madness, but rather a message about the dying values some of us as husbands, mates, and even fathers share …

We live in a society of double standards; a system that has brainwashed us from our youth to our adulthood in the responsibilities we bear as being men …

To be honest with oneself is to see the defiling of our **Black Women** and not turning a deaf ear to their cries or contributing to the callus behavior that has perpetuated through society's senseless display of moral disorder toward her …

Look at her, brother.

Look into the eyes of the living proof of **GOD** and tell me what you see.

For in the **FATHER** lives the **Mother**, and in that union—*our earthly understanding of what makes life meaningful*—is what brings together the oneness that makes her being here the testimony of **GOD'S** eternal love …

Now, I want you to ask yourself the question and be honest with the answer you know is true.

You know you can't feel without her feelings or see without her eyes showing you the way.

You know you can't within the laws of probability ponder the infinite sorrow surrounding your own tears, because your pain won't allow itself to be isolated in the confines of your personal misery.

You have to rise above your problems.

Don't allow your issues to be so nonconforming to the perils of her plight that her wish for a better life should lie dormant or imprisoned in your mind.

Because within your woman lies the last testimony of Life.

The final wish she begs within the solitude of her soul that you as a man recover from your self-induced ignorance.

For she, being the nurturer of Life, is willing to show you the way.

If only you seek the answer through her.

The Message 2

As a child, our happiest and most tender moments were spent looking into the eyes of a woman, and as men, those same moments are made meaningful through the expression of love we experience from them …

Your woman is made from that same composition you called "mother," and your presence remains also in the spiritual union that created her name.

"… this is now bone of my bones, and flesh of my flesh; she shall be called Woman, because she was taken out of Man."

From the first womb, brother, you are the mother of her, because she was taken out of you …

I'll say this again, and I want you to be clear … I want you to be *very* clear….

From the *first* womb, you are the mother of her, because she was taken out of *you* …

It's not in the sight of your eyes to see the meaning of what I've said, nor can mere words fully incorporate it in the language of sound.

Only in the unconditional limits of your spirit, where age is no longer an issue defined by numbers, where a lifetime is only but a moment cycling itself around a completion too spiritual to comprehend, can you only *feel* into the infinity of what I've said …

She's from you, brother.

Her flesh and bones have a direct link to your biological composition, creating a composite sketch of what you can't see in yourself unless you look into her eyes …

And in that glance, the wholeness of your being is made real through your understanding of what makes her real.

And in that clarity, the crystallized moment that makes worth worthwhile becomes clear through your spiritual need in her existence, allowing you not only to *see*, but most importantly, to *feel* the total commitment of a man to his **womb-man**.

Be Aware

In these dog days of summer,
hardening facts will stand at the doorway of your
soul.
Always be mindful of the truth you've
seen and heard,
and never … never answer the door
without knowing what's on the other side.

Dawn's Fear

The dawn peeks out, paranoid of its own presence. It seeks shelter from the light it shines our way, as the drug war boldly moves from the still of darkness to the dawning of a new day.

The Streets

I surveyed the aftermath of the battle zone: *the streets of a quiet neighborhood shattered by the sounds of gunfire.*

Bullets ricocheting, screams relating to the pain and suffering of a generation gone out of control.

The source, of which, my mind no longer connects a face with a name as the body count rises to a total obtained by another young person lying lifeless in the streets—*killed by a stray bullet marked for any soul that gets in its way* ...

The shock value to this incident registers on the scale of city life as 1.

One less legacy to worry about.

One less possibility of promise.

One less person to place the blame by a society refusing to acknowledge its own shame ...

How long, people, how long?

How long can we allow the death of a generation to be linked to its own origin?

As the substance in which they've placed their

values hampers their ability to judge the true worth of living.

Rejecting self and siphoning their hatred through a funnel too narrow to fill their cups with the understanding necessary to quench their thirst for togetherness, they, instead, rebel against each other.

Fighting over a turf that has no territorial boundaries, for Satan has enlarged their greed so that they can never be satisfied.

Filling their pockets with money and placing in their hearts the love for more money, their search ends where their greed begins as the bloodstained dollars bear a constant reminder of the service rendered by the death of another friend ...

Is *this* what we've reduced ourselves to?

Has *this* become the trade-off for living without fear—

Allowing a treasure as precious as our young to die without knowing why **GOD** has them here.

IX

Time ticks slowly into tomorrow
with the reluctancy of seeing another day,
as our young face their morning with sorrow,
for another friend died yesterday.

The Truth That Lives Inside Our Young

We know what lives inside our young—that which breeds a continuation of suffering.

For the scars of racism have cut deep into their veins, causing to spew from their bodies the fluid of tolerance: *out upon the streets of Park Heights, North Avenue, and Pulaski, past the stage of pacified protesters.*

They have no other recourse but to fight ***that*** which prohibits ***them*** from sustaining ***self***.

Eliminating, as they go, the lies taught to them during their journey; for they are now traveling their road to redemption, purged by the salty waters of Struggle's last attempt to bring them down …

Their dissatisfaction is symptomatic of their way of living as the simpler things evade their reach, forcing them to give up on society and its system of justice, unlike we who accept it.

The only problem is they have no direction.

The ability to see beyond the horizon crowned with the understanding of the past.

That was our obligation to them, to prepare and nurture their minds, giving them the insight necessary to take on the forces that stand between them and their love for themselves.

They, instead, feed upon an anger that lives inside us all, destroying the outer shell from an inner rage gone wrong as their emotions override the logic necessary to cope with the problem causing their downfall …

We can't run from ourselves as our reflection stands before us in the image of our young: *the adolescence of our adulthood acting out the anger we all inwardly feel.*

For they are our future left to carry on the responsibility of leading the next generation into a better life.

But what have we left them to build upon? What hope have we instilled inside their dreams?

Think about it, brothers and sisters, think about it very carefully and answer it accordingly.

X

We watch every day the erosion of our moral fiber, which, through physical aggression, has canceled out collective bargaining, making the means to a disagreement the end result of another young person's life ...

We can't stand idly by and allow this to continue.

If we do, a portion of our children will be cut off, eliminating in the twinkling of an eye the legacy of our labor.

A Memo to the Inquisitor

Since we can no longer fight for ourselves, **HE** has commenced **HIS** retaliation against you for us, releasing **HIS** instruments of destruction for the total annihilation of the Inquisitor, judging you for judging the worth of **HIS** people …

Choosing for the common good of the planet, **HE** has laid to rest the whys; for you no longer retain the right to stand before **HIM** as leaders.

As our cries reach the heights of **HIS** heavenly home, the soldiers of freedom are now on their way.

Lost in the Eye of the Hurricane

We're lost in the eye of the hurricane,
where the sunshine meets the rain,
Where the blue skies surrounded by cloudiness
spread destruction, poverty, and pain.

We're lost in the eye of the hurricane,
with no visible place to go,
hating ourselves and one another,
not understanding who's really the foe.

We're lost in the eye of the hurricane.
Beam your light, **FATHER** so we can see.

Understand, my people, the storm is the center,
the center of our misery.

We've been lost for a long time now,
and we're trying to find our way home.

Back to a place that has missed us dearly.
Back to land we've never known.

Look to the Father

*Don't close your heart to **GOD**.*

*Allow **HIM** to come in and realize **HIS** presence, and with open arms, welcome **HIM** welcoming you, and to each other, give thanks for your reunion: you to **THE FATHER**, and **THE FATHER** to you ...*

At this point, your direction becomes clear.

Even though the road of life is sometimes rough, your mission must maintain, because in your heart, you know **GOD** is truly wonderful.

And the knowing of this is all you will need to return to **HIS** source—that's where your commitment begins.

For the mere act of survival is no longer an issue.

What becomes important is who do you live for? And what purpose does your being here play in your search to find an answer ... a reason?

*Feel into the chambers of **GOD'S** love and make your assessment based upon the truth that lives inside **HIS** holy name, and in **HIM** find peace in yourself.*

You Can Do It

Do now what must be done.
Make your need to succeed outweigh Failure's
ability to turn you away.
For what lurks in front of you is a point you've
already passed, and your only liability lies in your
inability to learn from the past.

My Pledge

I make this pledge to the governing force of **GOD**, to stand firm in the foundation of existence, fighting with the forces that plot outside of me.

Taking charge of my body, this temple which my spirit calls home, cleansing it of the pollutants heaved upon me to conform.

No longer will I allow myself to be dictated by policies and principles that are impartial to my spiritual growth.

*For that which lives in me, the gift **GOD** has given me, refuses to acknowledge the virtues of life as defined by a dying creed.*

My well-being depends on the nurturing care of the mother-fatherhood instilled inside of me, and the intuitive knowing of **GOD**-sense which Eve plucked as a fruit from a tree.

With these tools, the administering hands of faith can now make whole this heartless shell of a man called me.

XI

Stand before your brother and sister,
extend your arms in open friendship,
looking not for a reward for your gesture,
but rather,
for the peace that allows your heart to heal.

XII

The sins done on the Sabbath
cannot be sanctified on a Sunday.

Final Word

The sensitivity of a man speaks to you.
The sensitivity of a man speaks through you.
The sensitivity of a man speaks for you,
and sometimes,
the sensitivity of a man speaks against you.
But most importantly,
the sensitivity of a man loves you.
This book you have just read,
if there is no other gift in life for me to give,
I entrust it to you.

Anyone wishing to contact me
can do so on Facebook @
The Sensitivity of a Man,
or
Quietnite2@aol.com.

Thank you, and may **GOD** bless you
and keep you embraced in **HIS** loving arms.

224063LV00004B/28/P

9 781432 753016